Cool cats

City Cats

Hello, Mr. Tibbles.

what are you looking so pleased about?

# Happy Cats!

cats sleep...

z<sup>z</sup>z<sub>z</sub>zz

all day long!

Pretty Patterned Kitten

Welcome to the **crazy cat family!**

Oh my! You're such a pretty kitty!

# Doodle Cats

A Crowd of Cats.

Cats love butterflies.

we

love

you!

# Understanding your new feline friend:

## Confused

## Just chillin'

## Hungry

## Happy

Jungle cat likes to . . .

pounce!

Flower Power.

# what Cute faces!

Hello, friend!

Can you count the kitty cats?

I love my **big** sister.

# Science Cat.

2+2

E=mc²

Look how smart he is!

where have you been?

Cats like to play hide and seek!

# Festive cats.

Pretty pattern.

what's kitty up to?

On the catwalk.

I love you,
kitten.

Flower Kitties.

Aren't I just the cutest?

Love Cats

# Bubbles the Cat.

# Hello, Grandad cat.

# Flora

loves flowers.

BESTEST

friends
forever.

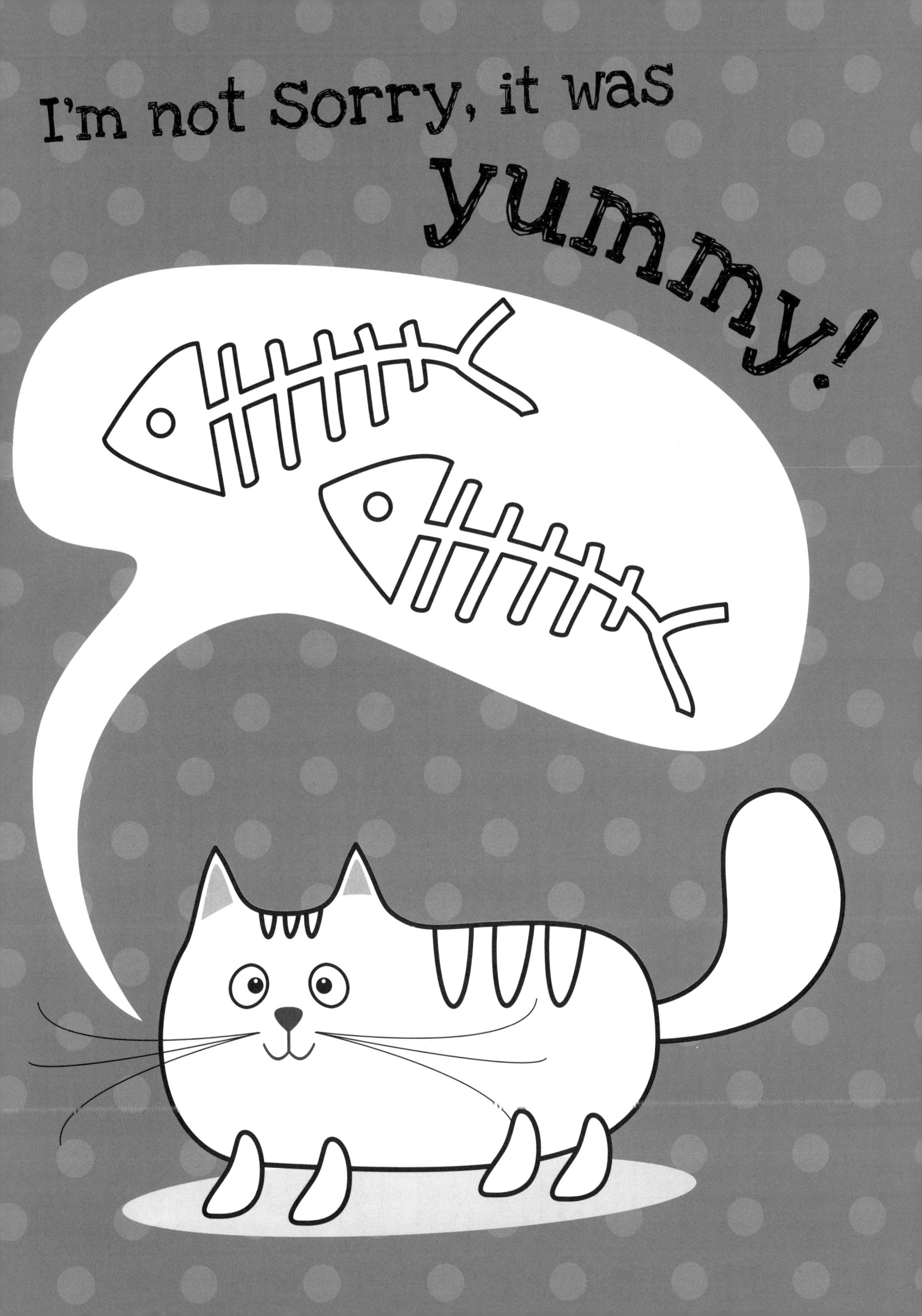
I'm not Sorry, it was
yummy!

Go away! I want to be

alone.

# Eight little cat faces.

# waiter cat

MENU

What would you like?

Streetwise cats

wash.

sleep.

Oh, hello there!

# Dapper cats
## like to get dressed up.

Don't they look fancy?

# Sailor Cat

# Wrap up warm!

It must be love!

Please feed me!

Cute as a button.

I love you, kitties!

The
best dressed
couple

in
town.

One cat,

two cats,

three cats!

I can see you!

Please could you **Cook** this for me?

# cats = love.

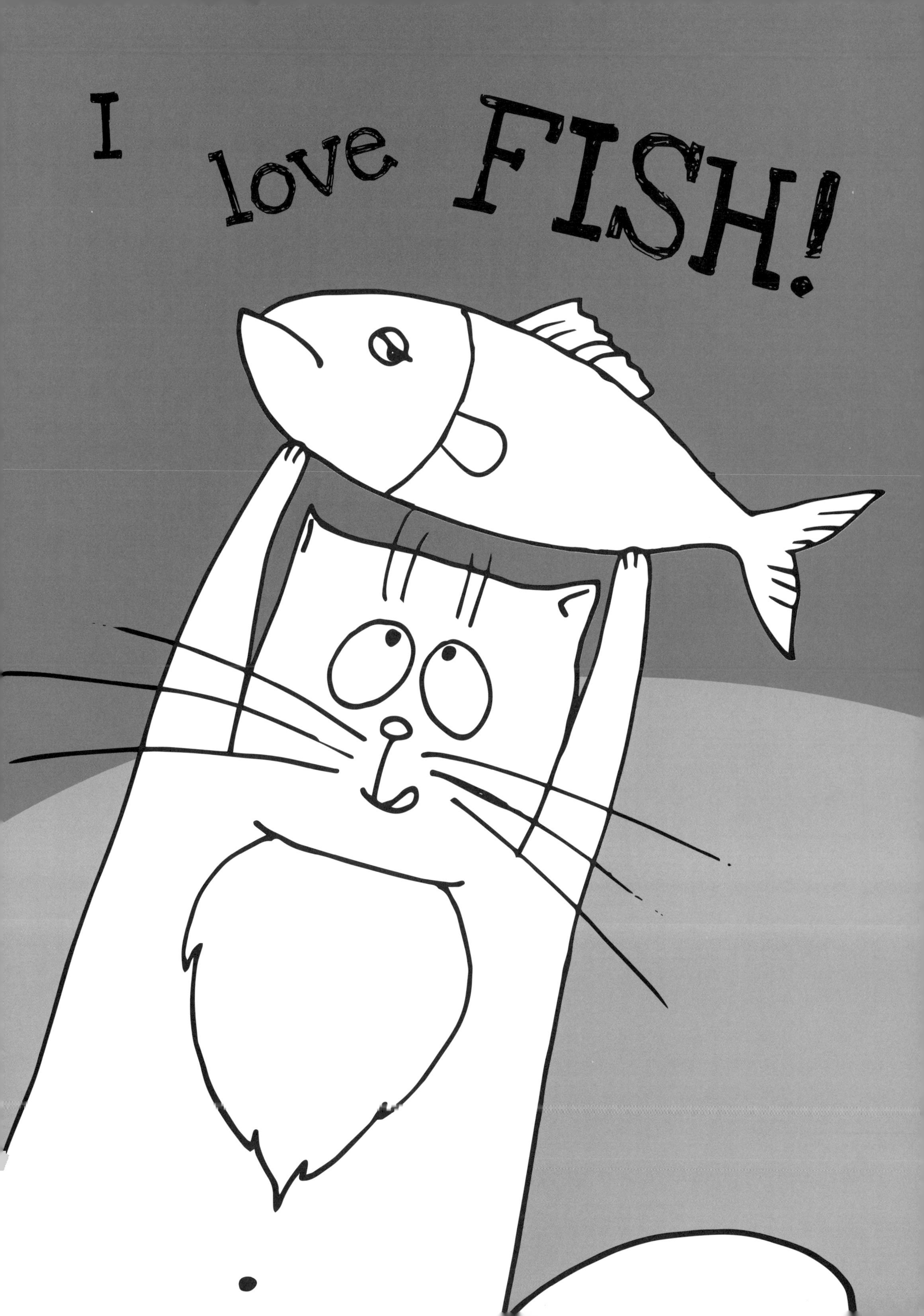
I love FISH!

# PuSS in boots

There never was a happier **happier**

kitty.

Purrfect

Cute Cat

Beautiful Cat